A GIFT FOR:

....

FROM:

....

Art Director: Chris Opheim
Editor: Theresa Trinder
Designer: Laura Elsenraat
Production Designer: Dan Horton

Copyright © 2015 Hallmark Licensing, LLC

Published by Hallmark Gift Books,
A division of Hallmark Cards, Inc.,
Kansas City, MO 64141
Visit us on the Web at Hallmark.com.

ISBN: 978-1-59530-786-6
1BOK2227
Made in China
0318

NOW YOU'RE
70!

MILESTONES & MEMORIES FOR YOUR GENERATION

By Brandon M. Crose

> "I HAVE ACHIEVED MY SEVENTY YEARS IN THE USUAL WAY, BY STICKING STRICTLY TO A SCHEME OF LIFE WHICH WOULD KILL ANYBODY ELSE…"
>
> —Mark Twain

America's "TV Generation" has seen the most dramatic changes in politics and culture of any generation before or since. You were raised in a time of post-war growth, prosperity, and the very real threat of nuclear annihilation. You came of age amidst war, protest, and revolutionary music. You remember a time before personal computers, where you were when JFK was shot, and your first color television. (You may be trying to forget the Disco Era, but you were there for that, too.) Most significantly, your story is also the story of how much America has changed since World War II. And it wasn't all Woodstock…

WHEN YOU WERE BORN...

IN THE NEWS

President Truman, on fear of Communist agents and sympathizers having infiltrated the U.S. government, ordered a loyalty probe of all federal employees. Though the probe was not awfully productive, it did appease some of Truman's criticizers, who believed that his administration was "soft on Communism."

If your family read the *Chicago Tribune*, they probably thought that Thomas Dewey beat Harry Truman in the 1948 Presidential election. The November 3rd issue went to press before all results were in—Truman, of course, was the victor.

A changing world: the United Nations was founded, an "iron curtain" fell across Berlin, and Chairman Mao proclaimed the People's Republic of China.

WHEN YOU
WERE BORN

At the announcement of V-J Day, hundreds of thousands of revelers crammed into Times Square to celebrate the end of World War II.

Inspired by "Rosie the Riveter," several million women excelled at jobs that were traditionally male only, helping to build the ships, tanks, planes, and guns that were needed to win the war. And for the first time, women were also allowed to join the four military branches as auxiliary support. More than 300,000 served as "soldiers in skirts"— SPARS, WASPS, WACS, and WAVES.

The invention of the atomic bomb and the subsequent annihilation of two Japanese cities, Hiroshima and Nagasaki, definitively ended the war and gave birth to an atomic age of boundless scientific achievement. Suddenly, anything was possible…even the end of the world.

More than 1.5 million African-Americans had served in the war, and many had been promoted to officer ranks. Long-held racial divisions were breaking down—and eventually led to President Truman's 1948 order to desegregate U.S. armed forces.

WHEN YOU WERE BORN

MUSIC

You may not remember now, but "Zip-a-Dee-Doo-Dah" from *Song of the South*, "The Woody Woodpecker Song" by George Tibbles and Ramey Idriss, and "A: You're Adorable" by Perry Como with the Fontane Sisters were likely to be among the first songs you ever heard.

Jazz and bebop were still big, and after performing with other legends such as Dizzy Gillespie, Miles Davis, and Fats Navarro, Billy Eckstine became a tremendously popular solo artist, rivaling even Ol' Blue Eyes with hits like "Everything I Have Is Yours."

Two perennial holiday favorites hit the airwaves for the first time: Gene Autry's "Rudolph the Red-Nosed Reindeer" and "All I Want for Christmas Is My Two Front Teeth" by Spike Jones and His City Slickers.

WHEN YOU WERE BORN

If your family lived near New York City and were the theatergoing type, perennial musical theater favorites *Annie Get Your Gun*, *Brigadoon*, and *Kiss Me, Kate* all made their Broadway debut during this time.

NOW SHOWING:

A WALK IN THE SUN
THE SONG OF BERNADETTE
IT'S A WONDERFUL LIFE

MOVIES

Silver screen and box office stars of the day included Bing Crosby, Ingrid Bergman, Clark Gable, Betty Grable, Bob Hope, Judy Garland, Humphrey Bogart, Greer Garson, and Spencer Tracy.

A movie ticket was only $0.35 and, on a Saturday matinee, a ticket would have bought your parents two movies; newsreels; an episode of a weekly serial such as *Jungle Raiders* or *Chick Carter*, *Detective*; and a cartoon.

Your parents may have seen one of the many popular war movies of the time: *The Story of G.I. Joe, They Were Expendable, A Walk in the Sun,* and the multi-Oscar-winning *The Best Years of Our Lives*, which featured a moving performance from real-life disabled veteran Harold Russell.

The first-ever Golden Globe Awards honored *The Song of Bernadette* with Best Picture, Best Actress in a Leading Role (Jennifer Jones), and Best Director (Henry King). Later Golden Globes recognized other notable movies you might remember: *Going My Way, The Bells of St. Mary's,* and *It's a Wonderful Life*.

WHEN YOU WERE BORN

TV AND RADIO

As with refrigerators and stoves, the production of new television sets was banned during the war, so they were rare and expensive—a staggering $700! However, production of more affordable sets, like the RCA 10-inch ($374), began in earnest after the war was over, and by the end of the decade, 4.2 million homes had a television set.

Researchers at Bell Telephone Laboratories invented the transistor, a tiny gadget that revolutionized modern electronics and eventually gave you your transistor radio!

So radio remained king, and your parent's standards probably included *Ma Perkins, Red Skelton, Fibber McGee and Molly, Twenty Questions, Jack Benny,* and *Lux Radio Theater.*

"Soaps" remained the most popular daytime radio program, with *The Guiding Light, Woman in White, Road of Life,* and *Right to Happiness* leading the pack. You may not have known this, but one woman—Irma Philips—wrote all of these programs.

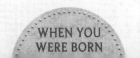

WHEN YOU
WERE BORN

If your family was one of the first in your neighborhood to purchase a TV (or you were friendly with a neighbor who did), you probably saw the first television broadcast of a World Series—the New York Yankees versus the Brooklyn Dodgers.

SPORTS

Created to maintain national interest in baseball while male players like Ted Williams and Joe DiMaggio were away at war, the All-American Girls Professional Baseball League proved that female sports players could also draw a crowd. The league had more than 900,000 attendees at its peak, years after the war had ended and the men returned.

Right out of college, George Mikan—at a dominating 6 foot 10 inches— led the Chicago American Gears to the 1947 National Basketball League title.

Jackie Robinson broke professional baseball's color barrier by becoming the first African American to play Major League Baseball since 1889 and then made history *again* by earning Rookie of the Year for his first season.

The Games of the XIV Olympiad (or, less formally, the 1948 Summer Olympics in London) were the first of your lifetime. Owing to the outbreak of war, they had been suspended since the 1936 Summer Olympics in Berlin. The United States dominated with 84 medals, 38 of them gold.

WHEN YOU
WERE BORN

Richard and Maurice McDonald opened the first McDonald's restaurant in San Bernardino, California. The walk-up stand sold hamburgers for $0.15—half the price as many other restaurants.

POP CULTURE

Food rationing did not end immediately after the war, and it would be several years more before the economy began to experience a boom. But one thing was "booming": babies! You were among the very first of a large generation that would shape American culture and policy like no other.

Parents were most likely to name their baby boys James, Robert, John, William, or Richard. Their baby girls: Mary, Linda, Barbara, Patricia, and Carol.

Whatever your parents named you, you were likely to have been one of the first children raised on the advice of Dr. Benjamin Spock. He published his first book, *The Common Sense Book of Baby and Child Care*, in 1946.

Minimum wage was $0.40 an hour, and the average annual salary was about $3,300. A postage stamp was $0.03, a loaf of bread was $0.10, and if they had the means, a new Rolls-Royce convertible would have cost your parents $18,500.

WHEN YOU
WERE BORN

WHEN YOU WERE A KID...

IN THE NEWS

Senator Joseph McCarthy's wild accusations of Communist sympathizers and spies within the federal government amplified Cold War fear...until the Army-McCarthy hearings led to his fall from grace.

You still liked Ike! After a spate of health problems, President Eisenhower barely campaigned for his second term and handily won over Adlai Stevenson— 36 million votes to 26 million.

You can thank Sputnik for all the math and science you had to take in school. The Soviet launch of the world's first artificial satellite started a space race, and everyone had to do his or her part to ensure American victory.

Though you were too young to apply for an account, perhaps your parents had one of the very first credit cards, The Diner's Club, available in the early 1950s. (It was made out of cardboard, unfortunately, until the ever-popular plastic versions were manufactured about ten years later.)

WHEN YOU
WERE A KID

The Civil Rights Movement won a major victory in *Brown v. Board of Education*, with the Supreme Court ruling at last that segregation in public schools was unconstitutional.

EVENTS

The U.S. Navy launched the world's first nuclear-powered submarine: the U.S.S. *Nautilus*. Since it did not run on diesel like its predecessors, it could remain submerged for almost indefinite periods.

At the height of the polio epidemic in America—more than 57,628 new cases were reported in a single year—Jonas Salk finally introduced a successful vaccine. The crippling disease, which had affected mostly children but sometimes adults, would become almost nonexistent within the decade.

Scientific advancements seemed to belong more to science fiction than reality: America and the Soviet Union both successfully tested intercontinental ballistic missiles, Sputnik I and then II circled Earth, and an early test of the hydrogen bomb at Bikini Atoll was estimated to burn five times hotter than the sun's core.

WHEN YOU
WERE A KID

MUSIC

If you were one of the very first to enjoy music on your sleek, light, and durable transistor radio, you might have owned a Regency TR-1 or a Raytheon 8-TP-1. At a princely sum of $49.95 for the TR-1 and $79.95 for the 8-TP-1, though, your parents likely waited for future, more reasonably priced models—like the Sony TR-63.

For now, you probably listened to new hits by Jackie Gleason, Glenn Miller, Bill Haley and the Comets, Frank Sinatra, and a young Elvis Presley through your family's radio or record player.

A Cleveland, Ohio disc jockey named Alan Freed (or "Moondog") coined the term "Rock 'n' Roll"— a combination of rhythm and blues and country and Western music. It is "a river that has absorbed many streams," Freed would say later in a movie called *Rock, Rock, Rock*. "All have contributed to the big beat."

Some of your other favorite songs might have included "Hernando's Hideaway" by Archie Bleyer, "The Ballad of Davy Crockett" by Fess Parker, and "Qué Será, Será" by Doris Day.

WHEN YOU WERE A KID

NOW SHOWING:

OLD YELLER

REBEL WITHOUT A CAUSE

IT CAME FROM OUTER SPACE

MOVIES

You may have seen Disney classics *20,000 Leagues Under the Sea, Lady and the Tramp,* and *Old Yeller* when they were first in the theaters. The *New York Times*, by the way, called *Old Yeller* "a warm, appealing little rustic tale," but children of the late 50s would never forget its heart-wrenching climax.

Young explorers were first introduced to the mysteries of the aquatic deep through Jacque Cousteau's *The Silent World.*

James Dean, icon of teenage rebellion, made only three movies—*East of Eden, Rebel Without a Cause,* and *Giant* (released posthumously)— before his untimely death at the age of 24.

If you were lucky, your first movie experience may have been in 3D, which was all the rage in the early 50s, as studios tried to entice families to leave their home television sets. Some of the most memorable were *It Came from Outer Space, Creature from the Black Lagoon,* and *Revenge of the Creature* (which happened to be Clint Eastwood's film debut).

WHEN YOU
WERE A KID

TV

Daniel Marsh, then-president of Boston University, had remarked, "If the television craze continues with the present level of programs, we are destined to have a nation of morons." He must not have missed such intellectual programming as Rod Serling and Paddy Chayefsky's *Marty*, which is now considered to be the *Citizen Kane* of TV, or Edward R. Murrow's *See It Now*, which did the unthinkable by challenging Senator McCarthy's culture of fear.

But sometimes TV was just relaxing. Maybe you enjoyed your convenient and modern TV dinners on folding TV tables while watching *Disneyland*, *I Love Lucy*, *The Jackie Gleason Show*, *You Bet Your Life*, *The Ed Sullivan Show*, or *The $64,000 Question*.

You may have even been one of the 30 million viewers to watch the wedding of celebrity actress Grace Kelly to Prince Rainier III of Monaco.

WHEN YOU
WERE A KID

By the mid 50s, Americans were buying an average of seven million TV sets per year. Approximately one in seven American families owned at least one television, and the typical viewer spent 42 hours per week watching it!

SEPTEMBER 19, 1955

SPORTS
RATED

ROCKY THE CHAMP

IN THIS ISSUE:
HOW ARCHIE
PLANS TO BEAT HIM

25 CENTS
$7.50 A YEAR

SPORTS

Mickey Mantle's hallowed Triple Crown season included .340 batting and 52 home runs, helping the Yankees clinch the pennant against the Dodgers.

**Heavyweight champion
Rocky "The Rock" Marciano
retired from boxing at the age of 31,
undefeated. He won 49 fights;
all but six of them ended in a KO.**

Jim Brown debuted with the Cleveland Browns, leading the league in his first year with 942 yards rushing (including a record-breaking 237 in one game against the Los Angeles Rams).

New York baseball fans lost not one but two teams when longtime rivals the New York Giants and the Brooklyn Dodgers both moved to California.

WHEN YOU
WERE A KID

POP CULTURE

Suburbia! Housing developments were everywhere—during 1957, a new home was built every seven seconds. Despite the sudden recession, the American Dream of home ownership was within reach.

Between April and September, the arrival of the Good Humor Man with his crisp white uniform and wide array of frozen confections probably caused a minor riot in your neighborhood. Your Good Humor bar cost a dime…unless you found a "free stick" in your last bar!

Your family may have had a fallout shelter in your basement or backyard for fear of a nuclear attack on American soil. The government encouraged this precaution, circulating pamphlets like "Six Steps to Survival" and "Facts about Fallout."

Old classics such as Tinkertoys, Lincoln Logs, and Erector Sets were still around, but you also had Candy Land, Chutes and Ladders, Clue, and Scrabble! New toys included Tonka Trucks and everyone's favorite science experiment gone wrong: Silly Putty ("invented" during the war when a General Electrics engineer tried to create a synthetic rubber).

WHEN YOU WERE A KID

WHEN YOU WERE A TEENAGER..

IN THE NEWS

In Alabama, racial violence raged: Freedom Riders were savagely beaten by white mobs in Birmingham, and martial law was declared in Montgomery after a crowd of both adults and children began throwing stones through the windows of a church where Dr. Martin Luther King, Jr. was speaking.

Fear of nuclear annihilation rocked the world for thirteen very tense days as superpower leaders President John F. Kennedy and Soviet Premier Nikita Khrushchev negotiated the Cuban Missile Crisis.

The public assassination of President John F. Kennedy became the defining moment of your generation. For many, it was the end of an era marked by innocence and optimism.

Whether you served or knew someone who did, you were touched in some way by the war in Vietnam. Nearly nine million served from 1964 to 1973, during which time over 58,000 Americans were killed and over 300,000 wounded.

WHEN YOU
WERE A TEEN

President Lyndon B. Johnson signed the Civil Rights Act with more than 75 pens—which he later bestowed upon congressional supporters and civil rights leaders, such as Hubert Humphrey and Martin Luther King, Jr.

The space race had just begun, and the Eco Movement was born: Rachel Carson's book *Silent Spring* warned (among other things) that the widespread use of DDT and other insecticides was exposing us to over 500 different kinds of chemicals.

Congress passed the Civil Rights Act, banning segregation in public places and employment discrimination on the basis on race, color, religion, sex or national origin.

In pursuit of his "Great Society," President Johnson passed even more landmark legislation, this time to reduce poverty, create affordable housing, protect the environment, provide government health insurance for the sick and elderly, and set standards for the quality of drinking water.

The birth control pill gave women the ability to plan or prevent pregnancy, and the Baby Boom came to an end.

WHEN YOU
WERE A TEEN

MUSIC

Even if you were not among the screaming teenagers pelting the "four lads from Liverpool" with jellybeans, you couldn't have missed The Beatles—they already had the top five spots on the Billboard Hot 100 singles chart before their first-ever American appearance on *The Ed Sullivan Show*.

When the unique sound of a Motown hit came on your car radio, you couldn't mistake it for anything else. The Detroit label launched the careers of many black musicians, including The Supremes, whose broad appeal landed them on the top of the Billboard charts twelve times.

Other familiar songs included "Shout! Shout! (Knock Yourself Out)" by Ernie Maresca, "Wipeout" by The Surfaris, and "Leader of the Pack" by The Shangri-Las.

WHEN YOU WERE A TEEN

You had probably never heard
of The Pendletones, but you
listened up when the band changed
its name to The Beach Boys—
"Surfin' Safari" and "Surfin' USA"
were Top 20 hits.

NOW SHOWING:

BREAKFAST AT TIFFANY'S

MUSCLE BEACH PARTY

PAJAMA PARTY

MOVIES

Once you had a car (or were able to borrow Dad's), drive-in theaters were still the place to be—and if yours charged admission by the carload rather than by person, they were still cheap, too!

You probably went to a drive-in with your sweetheart to "watch" some of the immensely popular beach party films that were out at the time, such as *Muscle Beach Party, Bikini Beach,* or *Pajama Party*.

Breakfast at Tiffany's, based on a novella by Truman Capote, made Audrey Hepburn a star, and influenced women's fashion nearly as much as Mrs. Kennedy's suits and pillbox hats. (The theme song, "Moon River," also won a Grammy.)

Your favorite stars may have included Doris Day, Frank Sinatra, Sandra Dee, Cary Grant, Elvis Presley, Elizabeth Taylor, Rock Hudson, Ann-Margret, Paul Newman, and Jerry Lewis.

WHEN YOU WERE A TEEN

TV

Many television firsts played a large role in John F. Kennedy's short presidency. You saw the first-ever televised presidential debate, which gave the more "telegenic" Kennedy a distinct advantage over Richard Nixon. You saw President Kennedy give the first live televised press conference. And JFK's assassination was covered in a level of detail like never before over the course of four days, which even included the first televised murder—that of Lee Harvey Oswald as he was being transferred to the Dallas county jail.

Alternatively, you may have started watching more football after your parents purchased a color TV set. The popularity of Sunday football soared once fans could see the color of their team's uniforms, and the Super Bowl was later created to give this growing audience something to cheer for.

You may have cooked your first omelet after seeing it done on TV. Julia Child made French cuisine accessible and interesting in *The French Chef*, which ran for ten years.

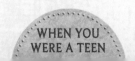

WHEN YOU
WERE A TEEN

SPORTS

Your parents saw Jackie Robinson break professional baseball's color barrier, and now you saw him become the first African American inducted into the Baseball Hall of Fame.

Jack Nicklaus defeated Arnold Palmer at the U.S. Open and won his first major tournament, but not his last— "The Golden Bear" went on to win a grand total of 73 PGA events during his long career.

Philadelphia Warriors basketball player Wilt Chamberlain scored a record-setting 100 points in one game to beat the New York Knicks 169–147.

You knew world heavyweight champion Cassius Clay to be brash and unpredictable. Still, many boxing fans were stunned when the world heavyweight champion converted to Islam and changed his name to "Muhammad Ali."

WHEN YOU WERE A TEEN

POP CULTURE

**Yours was the epitome of teenage culture—
you had disposable income, sleek automobiles,
drive-in theaters and restaurants,
Rock 'n' Roll, rebellion…and, probably
fairly often, parental disapproval.**

If you were extremely lucky, your first car may have
been a Ford Galaxie, Buick Riviera, or Chevrolet
Impala, but more likely, your father gave you his old
car—maybe a 1954 Plymouth Savoy Station Wagon?

Given a voice by Betty Friedan's book *The Feminine
Mystique,* many women began to question or reject the
role that popular culture had assigned to them, choosing
to pursue a career after school rather than settle down
immediately.

Inspired by the Free Speech Movement in Berkeley,
many students in college campuses across America
joined a rapidly growing youth movement to protest
unequal civil rights, poverty, and American involvement
in Vietnam.

WHEN YOU
WERE A TEEN

WHEN YOU WERE IN YOUR 20s...

IN THE NEWS

Kennedy's challenge to place a man on the moon was fulfilled, and you likely joined one billion other viewers (roughly one-fifth of the entire world's population!) to watch Neil Armstrong's historic "one small step."

You probably also remember the gripping seven-day saga of Apollo 13. An explosion crippled the shuttle's power, oxygen, and water supply, forcing the three astronauts to find a way to return home with very limited resources.

Called in to restore order, the Ohio National Guard fired upon anti-war protestors at Kent State University, injuring nine students and killing four.

The New York Times published top-secret documents that detailed U.S. involvement in Vietnam since World War II. Outraged, President Nixon formed a team called the "plumbers unit" to stop future government leaks—this same team would later break into the Watergate Hotel.

IN YOUR 20s

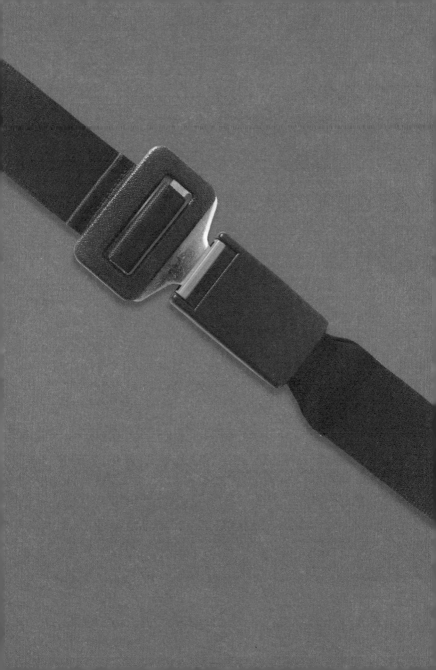

EVENTS

If you purchased a new car after 1966, it came equipped with seat belts (in all seats) and shatter-resistant windshields. Consumer advocate Ralph Nader's book *Unsafe at Any Speed* played a large part in making these safety standards law.

Perhaps you were among the 20 million people to take Wednesday off from work to celebrate the first Earth Day. Growing national interest in our environment soon paved the way for the Clean Air and Clean Water Acts.

Roe v. Wade: The Supreme Court controversially ruled it unconstitutional to deny women an abortion within the first trimester of pregnancy.

Technology seemed to be growing at an unchecked rate: a CAT scan could look inside your head, a space station called "Skylab" was orbiting the Earth, and computers started to get a lot smaller (and faster!) thanks to the microprocessor chip.

IN YOUR 20s

MUSIC

Revolutionary music—such as John Lennon's "Give Peace a Chance," James Brown's "(Say It Loud) I'm Black and I'm Proud," or Creedence Clearwater Revival's "Fortunate Son"—both reflected and fueled the times. Perhaps Bob Dylan had said it best: "You better start swimming or you'll sink like a stone, for the times they are a-changin'."

So much more than a concert, Woodstock was "Three Days of Peace and Music," and featured legends like Janis Joplin, the Grateful Dead, and Jimi Hendrix (to name a few). Despite a last-minute change in venue, construction delays, traffic jams, and concession and toilet shortages, Woodstock was one of the most pivotal events in music history.

It was a time of departures and new directions: The Beatles officially broke up, and Diana Ross began her solo career with a self-titled album that contained the chart-topping hit "Ain't No Mountain High Enough."

By your late twenties, the Rock 'n' Roll of your teenage years had evolved—and not quietly. Heavy metal bands Led Zeppelin, AC/DC, Aerosmith, and Van Halen blew out their amps (and your eardrums); innovative rockers The Eagles and Fleetwood Mac changed the musical landscape; punk rockers The Sex Pistols, Patti Smith, The Velvet Underground, and The Ramones spoke more to younger kids' teenaged rebellion than, perhaps, to your current state of mind.

IN YOUR 20s

NOW SHOWING:

DIAMONDS ARE FOREVER
THE GODFATHER
THE EXORCIST

MOVIES

Movies like *M*A*S*H* and *Patton* looked at the consequences of war, romances like *Love Story* and *Summer of '42* were very popular, and whether for pure escapist fun or fear of an uncertain future, disaster movies like *Airport*, *Earthquake*, and *The Poseidon Adventure* were giant hits.

Perhaps *Diamonds Are Forever*, but this James Bond film marked Sean Connery's last appearance as Agent 007.

If you watched *The 45th Annual Academy Awards*, you witnessed the first use of the show as a political platform when Marlon Brando, winner of Best Actor for *The Godfather*, sent the president of the National Native American Affirmative Image Committee to refuse his Oscar.

You couldn't look at pea soup the same way again after seeing *The Exorcist*. Arguably the most terrifying horror movie ever made, its grotesque special effects actually caused heart attacks in some theaters.

IN YOUR 20s

TV

Walter Cronkite may have changed your mind about the Vietnam War his unflinching coverage and scathing commentary on the *CBS Evening News* influenced mainstream public opinion.

After you were inundated with cigarette ads during your childhood and teenage years, the last-ever cigarette commercial was broadcast during Johnny Carson's *Tonight Show,* one minute before new legislation banning them became law.

If you still had a black-and-white television set, you were not completely behind the times—by the early 70s, only half of America watched television in color. Either way you watched it, you probably tuned into a documentary called *The Selling of the Pentagon*…or any of the 250 hours of the Senate Watergate hearings.

Hit shows of your early twenties included *Rowan and Martin's Laugh-In, Gunsmoke, Bonanza, All in the Family, ABC Movie of the Week,* and *The Mary Tyler Moore Show.*

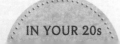

IN YOUR 20s

SPORTS

After a celebrated career that included 536 lifetime home runs and three American League MVPs, Mickey Mantle announced his retirement.

American swimmer Mark Spitz took home seven gold medals from the 1972 Munich Olympics, setting new world records in all seven events. Thanks to satellite TV, one billion viewers watched this joyous event—as well as the terrifying hostage crisis—live.

Billie Jean King scored a victory for women everywhere (and female athletes in particular) when she humbled Bobby Riggs in an exhibition tennis match billed as the "Battle of the Sexes."

Hank Aaron beat Babe Ruth's home run record of 714. And he didn't stop there—Aaron holds a total of 755 career home runs. In his own words: "I don't want them to forget Ruth; I just want them to remember me!"

POP CULTURE

During or after college, you may have completely horrified your parents by adopting an eclectic Hippy style: peace symbols, long hair, grungy jeans, fringed leather vests, mini skirts with chain belts, granny glasses…Anything goes!

Later, you may have joined in on the newest summer craze—string bikinis covered only the bare essentials (and only barely). They retailed for a pricey $35–$45.

Your first home probably cost you somewhere in the vicinity of $29,000. (Or you could have snagged the former home of Al Capone in Pine Hill, New Jersey, for $180,000, which was on the market about this time.)

Some now-familiar firsts included Starbucks opening its first coffee shop in Seattle, Gloria Steinem publishing the first issue of feminist magazine *Ms.*, and the Walt Disney World Resort in Florida welcoming visitors for the first time.

If you had boys, you were most likely to name them Michael, David, James, John, or Robert. If you had girls, they may have been Lisa, Jennifer, Michelle, Kimberly, or Melissa.

IN YOUR 20s

WHEN YOU WERE IN YOUR 30s...

IN THE NEWS

You and many others watched, helpless, as Iran militants seized sixty-six American citizens and held most of them hostage at a U.S. embassy in Tehran for over a year.

A partial meltdown at a nuclear power plant less than ten miles from Harrisburg, Pennsylvania (and one-hundred miles from Washington, D.C.) caused nationwide panic. Three Mile Island is now cited as the worst nuclear accident in American history.

"Where were you when the mountain blew?" Hopefully nowhere near it. Mt. St. Helens erupted with a force greater than 500 atomic bombs, killing 57 people and sending a drifting 16-mile-high plume of ash as far as Idaho and Montana.

Many Americans decided that they were not, in fact, better off than they were four years ago, and Ronald Reagan won the presidential election over incumbent Jimmy Carter in a historic landslide. The Reagan Revolution promised to restore "the great, confident roar of American progress and growth and optimism." And for many, it did.

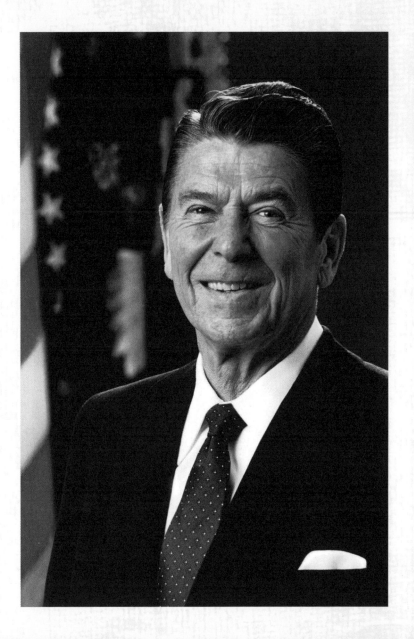

EVENTS

You were shocked by the assassination attempt on President Ronald Reagan, only 69 days in office, by John Hinckley, Jr.—and perhaps shocked again when the president returned to work a mere three days after a bullet pierced his lung.

While the rest of the country suffered from a deep recession, a growing technology boom (not to mention the nice weather) convinced many to relocate to the South and Southwest—these states saw a population increase of more than 25%!

Tired of the looming threat of nuclear disaster, and still shaken by the partial core meltdown at Three Mile Island, over one million people took to the streets of New York City to join the largest anti-nuclear demonstration in history.

Perhaps you owned one of the first Apple II computer systems? Soon after its debut, personal computers could be found in many homes. *Time* magazine even revised their "Man of the Year" feature to award the personal computer with "Machine of the Year."

IN YOUR 30s

Gender equality scored another victory when Arizona judge Sandra Day O'Connor became the first female U.S. Supreme Court Justice.

MUSIC

Danceable hits "Y.M.C.A." by the Village People and "We Are Family" by Sister Sledge personified a briefly lived "Disco Era," a time marked by lit floors, flashing lights, and polyester.

If you had $900–$1,000 to burn, you may have purchased a Sony CDP-101—the world's first commercially released CD player.

Think the title track to Bruce Springsteen's hit album "Born in the USA" is about American pride? Many did, and still do. However, "The Boss" wrote the song about how shamefully Vietnam veterans were treated after the war ended.

Other hit songs you might remember: The Knack's "My Sharona," Diana Ross and Lionel Richie's "Endless Love," and Pink Floyd's "Another Brick in the Wall, Part II."

MOVIES

Blockbuster popcorn flicks reigned supreme. You and your kids probably saw *Return of the Jedi, Ghostbusters,* and of course *E.T., the Extra-Terrestrial* in the theater. (You may have left the younger kids at home for *The Terminator*, though.)

You were much too young to remember when Mohandas Gandhi was assassinated, but Richard Attenborough's three-hour epic capably filled you in. *Gandhi* swept the Academy Awards, winning nine in total, including "Best Actor" for Ben Kingsley.

Burt Reynolds, Jane Fonda, John Travolta, Sally Field, Clint Eastwood, Sissy Spacek, Harrison Ford, Barbra Streisand, Dustin Hoffman, and Goldie Hawn were the leading stars of the day.

"Movie night" didn't always mean going to the theater—now all you had to do was rent a VHS tape from your local video store and pop it into your VCR. (Let's hope you didn't forget to rewind!)

IN YOUR 30s

Though they had been around for decades, soap operas—such as *Dallas, Dynasty, Knot's Landing,* and *Falcon Crest*—were suddenly appointment-viewing. An estimated two-thirds of all women with access to television tuned into at least one soap each day.

Now music was on your television, too! "Video Killed the Radio Star" by Buggles was, appropriately enough, the first music video played on MTV.

The final episode of *M*A*S*H* shattered TV records by drawing 105.97 million viewers. It held this record for 27 years— until 2010's *Super Bowl XLIV.*

At a time when the sitcom was considered dead, no one could have predicted the runaway success of *The Cosby Show*. It was the third most popular show in its first year, and *the* most popular show for the next four.

IN YOUR 30s

SPORTS

Canada hosted the Olympics for the first time in 1976. After the tragic events during the previous Games, tensions were high. South Africa was banned on account of its policy of apartheid, and several other African nations sat out in protest.

There was one truly perfect moment: Nadia Comăneci's perfect 10, the first in modern Olympics gymnastics history. And she didn't settle for just one—she left Montreal with seven perfect tens and three gold medals.

Muhammad Ali regained the World Heavyweight title from Leon Spinks after losing it to the former Olympic champion in a split decision.

Major League Baseball players went on strike over the issue of free-agent compensation. The strike lasted 49 days, resulting in the cancellation of 713 games.

After the strike was over, Cal Ripken, Jr. of the Baltimore Orioles played the first of 2,632 consecutive games—what would become a new record.

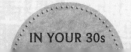
IN YOUR 30s

POP CULTURE

Trivial Pursuit was the hot new board game, cable television had a channel just for the weather, *USA Today* hit the newsstands, and Jane Fonda and Richard Simmons ushered in a fitness craze.

It was all about you! Self-help books, from *I'm OK, You're OK* to *You Can Negotiate Anything,* began to fly off the shelves.

You may have developed a healthy distrust of unnatural chemicals. Sales of health food rose from $140 million in 1970 to $1.6 billion in 1979!

On the other hand, by the time you turned 30, there were almost 7,000 fast food restaurants (compared to 3,400 just several years earlier). Is it any wonder that roughly 33% of meals were eaten out of the house?

WHEN YOU WERE IN YOUR 40s...

When you were a teenager, you saw the rise of the Berlin Wall, and now you saw it fall. With it, the Cold War came to a symbolic end.

IN THE NEWS

You probably still remember horrific images of wild birds covered in black oil. The Exxon Valdez, piloted by an inexperienced third mate, went off course and struck a reef in Alaska's Prince William Sound, spreading over 11 million gallons of crude oil over 1,300 miles of pristine coastline.

In fact, this decade saw shocking events both tragic and epic, including the Tiananmen Square massacre and the fall of the Soviet Union.

Still reeling from race riots after the Rodney King trial just two years earlier, Los Angeles was rocked by an early morning earthquake measuring 6.6 on the Richter scale.

Bill Clinton was the first president born after World War II and also the first Democrat to win reelection since Franklin Delano Roosevelt in 1944.

IN YOUR 40s

EVENTS

Arguably the most important dinosaur discovery of all time—the most complete Tyrannosaurus Rex skeleton was found—after only 65 million years—near Faith, South Dakota. "Sue" (named after the person who found her) rests her bones in Chicago's Field Museum.

Meanwhile, scientific advancements continued to bring you closer to science fiction: lasers were approved to perform precise eye surgery, your telephone went cordless, and you may have learned about black holes from Stephen Hawking's best-selling book *A Brief History of Time*.

People were checking e-mail, joining chat rooms, and browsing the Web on full-service programs like Prodigy, CompuServe, and America Online. If you had the means, you may have installed an extra phone line to "log on" without getting "booted" when the telephone rang.

Genetic modification allowed farmers to begin growing produce that was larger and more resistant to insecticides, though some scientists worried about the effects that these altered crops could have on the environment.

IN YOUR 40s

"STRAIGHT UP NOW TELL ME

DO YOU REALLY WANT TO LOVE, ME,

FOREVER, OH OH OH...

OR AM I CAUGHT IN A HIT AND RUN."

Paula Abdul–*Straight Up*, 1988

MUSIC

Remember all the torn jeans and baggy flannel shirts? Those kids probably listened to "grunge" bands like Nirvana, Pearl Jam, Soundgarden, Alice in Chains, or the Stone Temple Pilots.

A debut album by Dr. Dre, *The Chronic*, went platinum three times, bringing "gangsta rap" into the public eye and also launching the career of rapper Snoop Dogg.

Whitney Houston made her big screen debut with Kevin Costner in *The Bodyguard,* and the album (which featured her international chart-topping cover of Dolly Parton's "I Will Always Love You") became the best-selling soundtrack of all time.

Other familiar songs might include "Straight Up" by Paula Abdul, "Hold On" by Wilson Phillips, and "Gonna Make You Sweat (Everybody Dance Now)" by C & C Music Factory.

MOVIES

Denzel Washington starred in two landmark films—
as the slain civil rights leader in *Malcolm X* and as a
lawyer who fights to protect the rights of an HIV-
positive man in *Philadelphia*.

**Forrest Gump introduced the philosophy
"Life is like a box of chocolates" and gave
a new perspective to the memorable events
you experienced first hand.**

Everything old was new again. Movies based on the
radio and television shows of your youth included
Dennis the Menace, *The Fly*, and *Little Shop of Horrors*.

You probably also enjoyed *Thelma and Louise*, *The
Piano*, and the heartrending *Schindler's List*, which
earned a staggering 12 Academy Award nominations
and six Oscars, including Best Director and Best Picture.

IN YOUR 40s

NOW SHOWING:

FORREST GUMP
THELMA AND LOUISE
MALCOM X

. . . .

After hosting NBC's *The Tonight Show* for thirty years, Johnny Carson gave a tearful farewell to his fans when he retired from late-night television. And you were there to see it.

Perhaps you were also among the millions of people who saw the minute-by-minute televised coverage of current scandals—from the O.J. Simpson police chase and trial to the Tonya Harding/Nancy Kerrigan assault.

Nearly 60% of Americans spent most evenings on the couch, giving rise to the term "couch potato."

While on that couch, many potatoes enjoyed hit shows like *America's Funniest Home Videos*, *Home Improvement*, *Roseanne*, *The Golden Girls*, *Cheers*, and *Murder, She Wrote*. Or perhaps you became a fan of *The Simpsons*—the most successful animated family on primetime since *The Flintstones*.

SPORTS

Cincinnati Reds batter Pete Rose, after surpassing 4,191 hits to break a record set 57 years earlier by Ty Cobb, was ousted from baseball forever as a result of his illegal betting.

Three-time MVP Lakers player Earvin "Magic" Johnson, Jr. held an emotional press conference, announcing that he had tested positive for HIV, putting a new face on the AIDS epidemic.

Magic's announcement didn't stop the "Dream Team"—the first U.S. Olympic team to include NBA stars—from achieving Olympic greatness in Barcelona. "It was like Elvis and the Beatles put together...like traveling with 12 rock stars," claimed their coach, Chuck Daly.

Basketball was big news, but baseball fans were not pleased when a 257-day strike led to the cancellation of the 1994 year's World Series.

After stumbling in two previous Olympic competitions, American speed skater Dan Jensen exemplified perseverance by taking home the gold medal *and* setting a new world record in the 1994 Winter Olympics' 1,000-meter event.

IN YOUR 40s

The private lives of celebrities were suddenly matters of great interest. Supermarket tabloids—such as *Star, The Globe,* and *The National Enquirer*—sold by the tens of millions.

POP CULTURE

Dr. Deepak Chopra may have changed your mind about alternative medicine with his best selling book *Ageless Body, Timeless Mind*. If so, you weren't alone—*Time* magazine even named Chopra one of the Top 100 Icons and Heroes of the Century.

Plastic flowers danced to music, fanny packs were hip, books on tape let you read while driving, the much-disliked New Coke was replaced with Coca-Cola Classic, highly collectible Beanie Babies were *definitely* going to be worth a lot of money someday, and you learned that *Men Are from Mars, Women Are from Venus*.

If your children had children of their own, your grandson(s) might be named Michael, Matthew, Christopher, Jacob, or Joshua. Your granddaughter(s) might be named Jessica, Emily, Ashley, Samantha, or Hannah.

IN YOUR 40s

WHEN YOU WERE IN YOUR 50s...

IN THE NEWS

President William Clinton endured an impeachment trial over charges of grand jury perjury and obstruction of justice. He was narrowly acquitted on both counts.

Harkening back to *The Chicago Tribune's* gaffe of declaring "Dewey defeats Truman," many news stations prematurely reported Vice President Al Gore the winner of the 2000 Presidential election.

September 11th, 2001. We will never forget.

You'd witnessed the Challenger explosion, and you were saddened to see the second major disaster in the history of the space shuttle program as the space shuttle Columbia unexpectedly disintegrated after its return from a successful 16-day mission. All seven astronauts were killed, and the nation mourned... again.

IN YOUR 50s

EVENTS

If you hadn't yet gotten around to learning how to use a computer, you had even less incentive to do so now: the Y2K Bug threatened to send society back to the 1900s by exploiting an oversight in computers' internal clocks.

Previously a bulky thing for affluent people (or showoffs), the cell phone began to evolve by leaps and bounds.

Were you one of 50 million people without power during the Northeast Blackout of 2003? After a cascading power failure, eight U.S. states and parts of Canada were left without electricity for a day or longer.

The Human Genome Project—a massive undertaking by scientists from the United States, United Kingdom, Germany, France, Japan, and China—announced that it had finally mapped all known human genes.

A massive earthquake measuring 9.0 on the Richter scale loosed a disastrous tsunami on Southeast Asia, killing over 225,000 and displacing 1.2 million more.

IN YOUR 50s

Y2K

MUSIC

The way people listen to music has changed just as much as the music itself: from LPs to 8-tracks, and then cassette tapes to CDs, and finally to portable MP3 players like the Apple iPod, which could easily hold your entire music library.

With the option to buy music online by the song or album, digital downloads began to threaten sales of the physical CD. Tower Records, Virgin Records, and hundreds of independent record stores across the country began closing their doors.

Teen pop stars Christina Aguilera and Britney Spears "grew up," transitioning from more teen pop songs "Come On Over Baby (All I Want is You)" and "Oops!…I Did It Again" to more provocative hits like "Dirrty" and "I'm a Slave 4 U," respectively.

Whether or not you listened to them, Cher's "Believe," Faith Hill's "Breathe," and Alicia Keys's "Fallin'" were on the radio quite a lot.

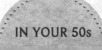

IN YOUR 50s

MOVIES

George Lucas released the long-awaited prequel to the original Star Wars trilogy of your thirties—*Episode I: The Phantom Menace*. Despite its mixed reviews, it was by far the top grossing film of its year.

Whether you read the books when they were first published, or just remember seeing "Frodo Lives!" on buttons and t-shirts later on, no one would deny that Peter Jackson's massively epic (and epically massive) *Lord of the Rings* film trilogy was the movie event of the decade.

Seabiscuit, starring Tobey Maguire and Jeff Bridges, chronicled the life story of a familiar underdog hero from your childhood years and was nominated for seven Academy Awards.

IN YOUR 50s

Thanks to her powerful performance in *Monster's Ball,* Halle Berry became the first African-American woman to win an Academy Award for Best Actress.

You may have watched
Candid Camera with Alan Funt,
but mega-popular shows such
as *Survivor* and *American Idol*
seemed to bear little resemblance
to the "reality TV" of your youth.

TV

You had to spring for the premium cable package (or wait for the DVDs) to catch some of the best shows on television, such as *The Sopranos, Six Feet Under, The Wire, The Shield,* and *Battlestar Galactica.*

If you tuned into the soap opera *All My Children* in your twenties or thirties, you probably felt justified to see Susan Lucci finally win an Emmy Award—after 18 unsuccessful nominations—for her role as Erica Kane.

Other popular shows you watched may have included *Who Wants to Be a Millionaire?, ER, Friends, Frasier, Law & Order, Everybody Loves Raymond, C.S.I.: Crime Scene Investigation,* and *Will & Grace.*

SPORTS

Having already become the youngest golfer to win the Masters Tournament—and by a record 12 strokes—Tiger Woods went on to set a new to-par record (−19) and then to become the first golfer ever to hold all four major championship titles at once.

NASCAR fans were stunned when seven-time Winston Cup champion Dale Earnhardt suffered a fatal crash during the final lap of the Daytona 500.

The 2002 Winter Olympics were held in Salt Lake City, with the United States setting a record for winning the most total medals at a home Winter Olympics, though Norway took home the most gold medals.

Long-beleaguered Boston Red Sox fans had their day when their team beat the St. Louis Cardinals to win their first World Series Championship in eighty-six years. The "Curse of the Bambino" was at last reversed!

POP CULTURE

You weren't imagining it: popular culture seemed obsessed with youth as advertisers trained their sights almost exclusively on teenagers. By the late 90s, teens were 31 million strong and willing to spend most of their money on music and movies...

Crocs were in, low-carb diets like Atkins were all the rage, young people were abuzz with energy drinks, and, after 9/11, it seemed that everyone had an American flag sticker on their car window or bumper.

Muggles of all ages made time to read about Harry Potter and his friends Ron and Hermione. J.K. Rowling's endearing books spawned several successful movies and a plethora of merchandise, but they were not loved by all—some schools banned the books for fear that they promoted witchcraft.

Medical breakthroughs were around every corner, and perhaps one of the most memorable—and profitable—was Viagra, netting $522 million in several months.
Now advertising for the drug is virtually everywhere, but you may remember the very first commercial, featuring former presidential candidate Bob Dole.

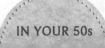

WHEN YOU WERE IN YOUR 60s...

IN THE NEWS

US Airways Flight 1549 was struck by a flock of geese shortly after takeoff, and Captain Chesley B. "Sully" Sullenberger became a national hero after making a crash landing in the Hudson River. Incredibly, no lives were lost.

An explosion on an oil rig fifty miles off the coast of Louisiana killed eleven workers and eventually resulted in the worst oil spill in U.S. history—an estimated 172 million gallons of crude oil permeated the Gulf coast...a disaster fifteen times greater than that of the Exxon Valdez.

Haiti was hit by a magnitude-7 earthquake, devastating the small Caribbean country and displacing 1.5 million people from their homes.

Almost 23 million Americans watched the royal wedding ceremony of Prince William and Kate Middleton, Duchess of Cambridge, at Westminster Abbey in London.

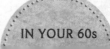

IN YOUR 60s

EVENTS

From humble beginnings to 44th President of the United States, Barack Obama showed the world that the American dream is very much alive.

The "Great Recession," which began with the collapse of AIG, Lehman Brothers, and Bear Sterns, made it difficult for young people to find a job or buy a house.

Despite popular fears that it could create a black hole in the middle of Western Europe, the Large Hadron Collider resumed operations, accelerating particles to previously unseen speeds in an attempt to learn more about the origins of our universe.

President Obama's controversial landmark bill—the Patient Protection and Affordable Care Act—passed in Congress and was signed into law, promising basic health insurance for everyone, regardless of age, sex, or preexisting conditions.

Fidel Castro, leader of Cuba since 1959, shocked the world by transferring his power to his baby brother, Raul, on account of his failing health.

IN YOUR 60s

MUSIC

After taking the world by surprise on *Britain's Got Talent*, Susan Boyle released her first album *I Dreamed a Dream*, which quickly became the second-best-selling album worldwide.

The world was stunned to learn that Michael Jackson died of a drug overdose less than a month before his sold-out concerts in London. Grieving fans bought 35 million of his albums, making Jackson the best-selling artist of 2009.

Coming full circle from the days of radio, online radio streaming services like Pandora gave anyone the ability to play a personalized selection of music through their computer.

Popular hit songs included "Poker Face" by Lady Gaga, "Firework" by Katy Perry, and "Hey, Soul Sister" by Train.

IN YOUR 60s

Superhero movies, many featuring characters that first debuted in comic books you may have read as a child, were everywhere! (And, by the way, if you have kept those comic books, they're probably worth a few dollars...)

Kathryn Bigelow became the first woman to win Best Director at the Academy Awards for *The Hurt Locker*, which depicted the story of a bomb-disposal team during the Iraq War.

The following year, *The King's Speech*, a British historical drama about King George VI overcoming his stammer in the time leading up to World War II (and shortly before you were born!), won four Oscars, including Best Picture, Best Actor, and Best Original Screenplay.

You may have also seen *The Blind Side*, *Up in the Air*, *The Town*, *Star Trek*, *The Fighter*, *Avatar*, *The Help*, or *My Week with Marilyn*.

TV

Remember when television sets were built into really heavy wooden cabinets? Most flat screen TVs are so light that they can be mounted on your wall.

One particular show was certain to bring back some memories. *Mad Men*—a period drama about the people who work at a New York advertising firm during the 1960s.

> **Music isn't the only thing that's gone digital—now you can watch TV shows on your computer, too!**

In fact, you probably heard that more and more people were canceling their expensive cable packages in favor of online streaming services like Netflix, Hulu, and Amazon Prime. Maybe you were one of them.

IN YOUR 60s

SPORTS

A long-delayed plan twenty years in the making, New York City finally opened two new ballparks in the same year—the New Yankee Stadium and Citi Field for the New York Yankees and the New York Mets, respectively.

The United States broke the record for the most medals won at a single Winter Olympics in 2010, with Americans Bode Miller and Shaun White having memorable breakout performances.

American cyclist Lance Armstrong survived cancer to take home seven Tour de France titles—only to have all of them stripped away after allegations of performance-enhancing drug use.

Tennis star Serena Williams made headlines for her angry outbursts at two separate U.S. Opens. The first cost her the match against Kim Clijsters, and while the second visibly rattled opponent Samantha Stosur, Williams still lost the Grand Slam title 6–2, 6–3 to Stosur.

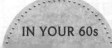

IN YOUR 60s

You remember a time before computers, and now they're an everyday part of life. For instance, you may use e-mail and popular social applications such as Facebook to keep in touch—and if you don't, everyone tells you you should!

POP CULTURE

Ah, retirement! Perhaps it's finally your turn? But just because retirees may not have had to get up for work anymore doesn't mean they had to stay home. By volunteering and staying active in the community, retirees were starting a "new chapter" in increasing numbers.

Perhaps you have wondered why celebrities your age are starting to look younger than you do? In many cases, the answer is Botox injections, which temporarily paralyze certain facial muscles, smoothing wrinkles and creating a more youthful (if somewhat puffy) face.

While many things have changed since the days of your youth, much has not. For instance, a quick look at the shelves of your local grocery store will reveal Ritz Crackers, Eight O'Clock Coffee, Morton's Salt, French's Mustard, Campbell's Tomato Soup, and Spam—all products that have been around since you were a kid!

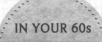

NOW YOU'RE 70!

And you're in good company!
Look who else is in their 70s:

- Ann-Margret, actress
- Reverend Jesse Jackson, activist and minister
- Pete Rose, baseball player and manager
- Martha Stewart, entrepreneur and television host
- Tom Selleck, actor
- Chubby Checker, musician
- Debbie Harry, singer
- Diane Sawyer, journalist
- Jim Davis, cartoonist
- Nancy Pelosi, U.S. Speaker of the House
- Sir Patrick Stewart, actor
- Muhammad Ali, heavyweight boxer
- Stephen Hawking, physicist
- Aretha Franklin, musician
- Garrison Keillor, radio personality
- Paul Simon and Art Garfunkel, musicians

"To be seventy years young
is sometimes far more cheerful
and hopeful than to be
forty years old."

—*Oliver Wendell Holmes, Sr.*

"These are the days
of miracle and wonder."

—*Paul Simon*

"There are no pleasures
in a fight but some of my fights
have been a pleasure to win."

—*Muhammed Ali*

DID YOU ENJOY THIS BOOK?

We would love to hear from you.

Please send your comments to:
Hallmark Book Feedback
P.O. Box 419034
Mail Drop 100
Kansas City, MO 64141

Or e-mail us at:
booknotes@hallmark.com